LIFT OFF!

This is Arthur the Alien. He's stuck on Earth and wants to go home. Fortunately he's come up with a cunning plan involving helium balloons.

I ♥ space

Sorry, got to fly!

D0318506

Arthur weighs the same as an average nine-year-old (28.6 kg). He needs around **2,043** helium balloons to lift him into the sky*.

*An average helium balloon can lift 14 g. To work out how many helium balloons you'd need to lift YOU, divide your weight in GRAMS by 14.

UP IN THE AIR

What might happen to Arthur as he rises through the sky? Start at the bottom and read UP!

THERMOSPHERE 80–1,000 km
At 2,000°C, temperatures are hotter than an oven here. But because the air is so thin, Arthur would feel freezing cold.

Northern lights

MESOSPHERE 50–80 km
Arthur's balloons would probably have burst by now. The highest a helium balloon has ever reached is 53 km. It's also –90°C here. That's colder than the South Pole!

Meteors

STRATOSPHERE 12–50 km
Air pressure would be so low here that Arthur would need a special pressure suit to stop the fluids in his body from boiling.

Weather balloon

TROPOSPHERE 0–12 km
The temperature would drop to about –57°C. Arthur would also need to breathe through an oxygen mask because oxygen levels would fall from 21% to 4%.

HYPER DRIVE

What if you could give Arthur a lift and just DRIVE him into space? How long would it take to get to different places?*

 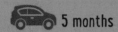 5 months

The Moon

  41 years

Venus

  93 years

Mercury

  152 years

The Sun

  228 years

Mars

  5,870 years ➔

(ANOTHER 24 PAGES)

Pluto

The fastest manned rocket ever – Apollo 10 – went at 25,000 mph. At THAT speed, you'd reach Mars in about 8 months and Pluto in about 16 years.

*Assuming you were going at 70 mph. And someone was driving the whole time. (No stops for a wee or buying crisps.)

FREE FALL

Uh-oh! Arthur's balloons have burst.
Luckily we've borrowed Luke Aikins' giant net.

WHO IS LUKE AIKINS?
He's an American skydiver. In 2016, he jumped from a
plane 7.6 km up in the sky **WITHOUT A PARACHUTE.**

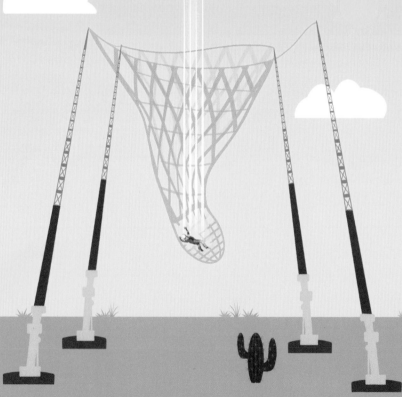

He landed in a huge net in the California desert
– and suffered NO injuries.

The net was 30 m² – about the size of four tennis courts.

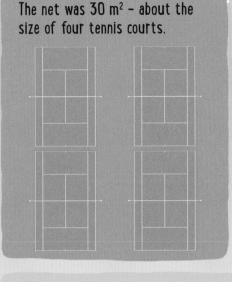

It was held up by four 61-metre cranes – taller than the Leaning Tower of Pisa.

Leaning Tower
57 m

Crane
61 m

As he fell, Luke Aikins reached speeds of 150 mph.

Fastest racehorse ever 44 mph

Fastest toboggan ever 84 mph

Fastest roller coaster  149 mph

Luke Aikins  150 mph

The net had to be deep – 20 storeys high – or Luke Aikins would have bounced straight out of it.

In 2012, Felix Baumgartner fell further (39 km) and faster (844 mph – breaking the sound barrier). But he used a giant parachute to slow himself down. I guess that makes him a... lightweight?

THIS IS A BLAST!

So you've decided to build a rocket in your back garden.
What do you need to think about?

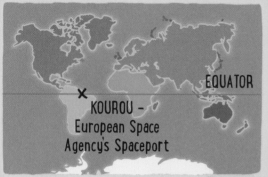

1. LOCATION

It would be good if your garden was near the Equator. The Earth spins fastest there, so rockets get an extra 'push' as they take off.

2. NOISE

It would help if no one were living next door. NASA's Saturn V made one of the loudest noises ever recorded – 220 db. This is loud enough to melt concrete.

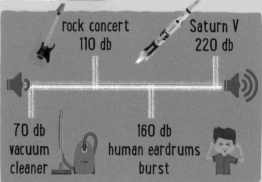

rock concert 110 db

Saturn V 220 db

70 db vacuum cleaner

160 db human eardrums burst

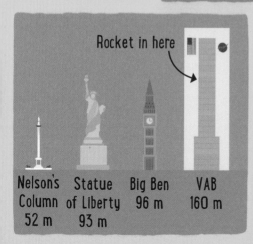

Rocket in here

Nelson's Column 52 m

Statue of Liberty 93 m

Big Ben 96 m

VAB 160 m

3. A LARGE SHED

You need to build (and store) your rocket somewhere. NASA's Vehicle Assembly Building (VAB) is the tallest single-story building in the world (160 m). It also contains the tallest doors (139 m).

SPACE SURVEY

People have strong views about space.
Which of these statements do YOU agree with?

53% of Americans say they'd like to go up
to space. Would you enjoy a space vacation?

One in ten British people say
they would be happy to go on
a ONE-WAY trip to Mars. That
means they'd NEVER get to
come back. Would you?

54% of people say they believe there is intelligent life on
other planets. Do you think aliens exist?

In a 2013 survey, 2.5%
of Americans said they had
been abducted or kidnapped
by aliens*. Do you believe
this is possible?

*Some people think the people in this survey might not have been telling the truth...

PACK IT IN!

Time to pack. There are no washing machines in space, so if you went for a year, you'd have to take THIS many pairs of pants.

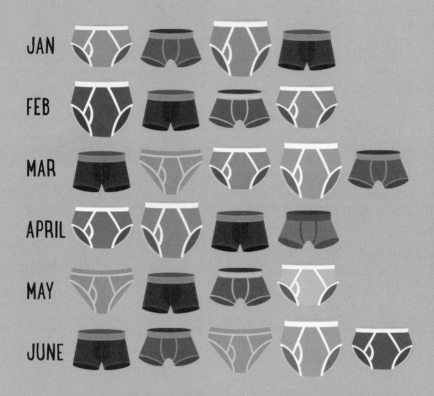

JAN

FEB

MAR

APRIL

MAY

JUNE

COSMIC PONG

Why only 52 pairs? According to cosmonauts on the Russian space station, Mir, they only changed their pants ONCE A WEEK. Science Officer Pettit of the International Space Station (or ISS) once wore the same pair of shorts for over THREE MONTHS.

PANTS ON FIRE!

What happens to the dirty undies? They become SHOOTING STARS. On the ISS, they are dropped into an old supply craft and ejected. Then, they burn up in the Earth's atmosphere.

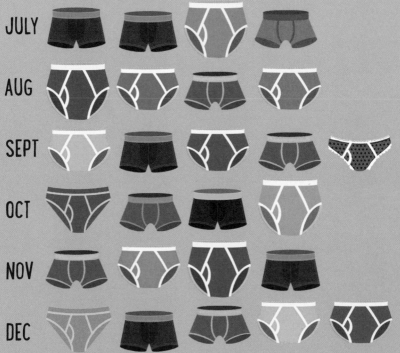

JULY

AUG

SEPT

OCT

NOV

DEC

HOME GROWN

Science Officer Pettit of the ISS once grew tomatoes in his old pants. He said: 'I figured there might be a few nutrients in there.' When he'd tried before, the seeds had got too cold and died, but in his magic pants, the seeds sprouted in two days.

AWESOME G-FORCE

When you take off in your rocket, you'll be subject to HUGE levels of G-force (which is measured in 'g's). But how much exactly?

DEFINITION
G-force = amount of force or acceleration acting on your body (or anywhere else).

KEY

 = 1 g

0 g	**1 g**	**3 g**	**5 g**	**5.2 g**
Weightlessness (like astronauts in space)	Normal gravity (like you're feeling now)	Space shuttle during launch	When most people black out	Olympic sledge (or 'luge')

ROCKET MAN
In 1954, John Stapp wanted to find out how much acceleration the human body could withstand.
He built a rocket sled that subjected him to 46.2 g – one of the highest levels ever. He suffered a total 'red out' (his eyes filled with blood) but made a full recovery and lived until he was 89.

6.3 g
Tower of Terror
roller coaster
(South Africa)*

7.2 g
Apollo 16 rocket

46.2 g
John Stapp
Rocket sledge

*You only feel 6.3 g for a few seconds, so the roller coaster is safe to ride!

WHAT A LOAD OF RUBBISH!

If you fly past the Moon, you might notice
something strange. 180 TONNES OF LITTER.

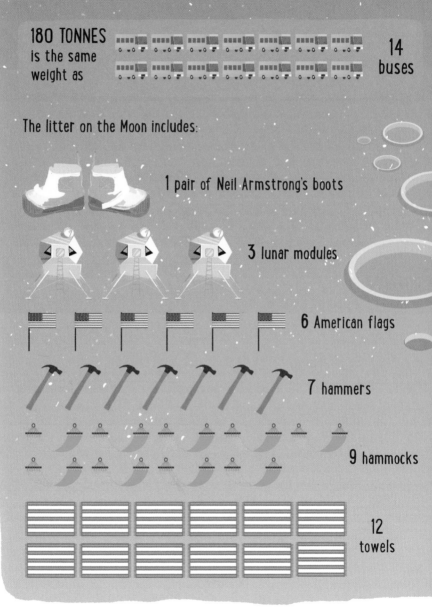

180 TONNES is the same weight as **14 buses**

The litter on the Moon includes:

1 pair of Neil Armstrong's boots

3 lunar modules

6 American flags

7 hammers

9 hammocks

12 towels

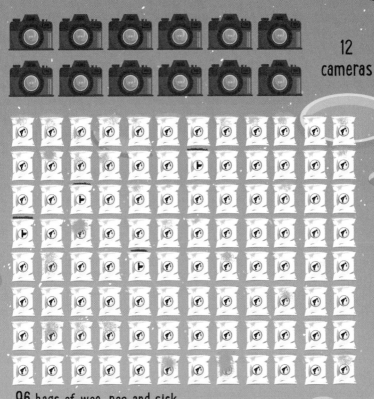

12 cameras

96 bags of wee, poo and sick

Plus **1000s** of footprints

WHY SO MUCH TRASH?

It's easier to get people and rockets UP to the Moon than to bring them back DOWN. So anything that isn't essential gets left behind.

WHY IS IT STILL THERE?

There's no wind or rain on the Moon to dissolve the trash or blow it away. A one-centimetre -deep footprint would take about 10,000 years to be filled in with moondust.

UP IN THE AIR

If you look out of your rocket window, you'll see our perfect planet. But it hasn't always looked like this.

SLIMEBALL
4.6 billion years ago

Earth was formed. For the next billion years, it was covered in a layer of slime with absolutely no life on it.

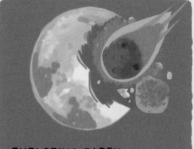

EXPLODING EARTH
4.5 billion years ago

A rock the size of Mars is believed to have smashed into Earth. A chunk fell off the Earth and became the Moon.

SNOWBALL EARTH
750–580 million years ago

During this period, temperatures dropped on Earth and scientists believed it was completely covered with snow and ice – like a giant snowball!

EARTH TODAY
The Earth is still changing

Europe and America move 2.5 cm further apart each year and global warming has shrunk the ice caps. What might Earth look like next?

BANG GOES YOUR SPACESHIP

Remember that not much of your rocket will survive its journey...*

Rocket when it takes off →

Rocket when it lands back on Earth →

So what happens to the rest of it?

THE BOTTOM BIT
Known as the 'first stage', this blasts the rocket into the sky, burning around 15 TONNES of fuel a second. It gets jettisoned after three minutes.

THE MIDDLE BIT
The rockets in the 'second stage' kick in after about three minutes. All the fuel is gone six minutes later and it is discarded too.

THE BOTTOM OF THE TOP BIT
The 'third stage' rockets usually get the astronauts to their final destination. This stage gets ditched in space.

OTHER STUFF
The tip gets ditched after three minutes. The other parts (like the lunar module) get dumped in space on the way back. The 111-metre rocket has turned into a 4-metre cone that splashes down in the sea.

*All calculations based on the rocket that took the astronauts to the Moon in 1969.

LIFE ON EARTH – PART ONE

Arthur the Alien has decided to make a scrapbook of his time on Earth. These two pages are about EARTHLINGS. He's got one fact wrong though. Can you spot the mistake?

At any one moment, around half a million people are in aeroplanes. And at least five people will be in space (usually on the International Space Station).

The Queen (or King) of England is the official owner of one-sixth of all the land on Earth.

Mine!

Around two-thirds of the world's people have never seen snow.

MOST COMMON BIRDS – TOP 3

Chicken	24 billion
Pheasant	173 million
Quail	168 million

The most common bird on Earth is the chicken because humans eat them (and their eggs).

65% of the world's population drive on the right-hand side of the road.

There are 268 people per square kilometre in the UK. There are three people per square kilometre in Australia.

Hello!

Bonjour!

¡Hola!

Ciao!

Salut!

Hallo!

Earthlings speak over 7,000 languages. The language of Ayapaneco is perhaps the rarest, with only two speakers left. For several decades, the two men refused to speak to each other, but they have now made up.

Antarctica is the smallest continent and has a population of around one million people.

People in Japan live the longest, with an average lifespan of 84 years. People in Sierra Leone have an average lifespan of just 50 years.

Which fact has Arthur got WRONG? Answer over here.

WEIGHT OFF MY MIND

if you stopped off on another planet, you'd notice that the gravity is a bit different. So let's say on Earth, you can lift a heavy suitcase (about 30 kg). What could you pick up on other planets?

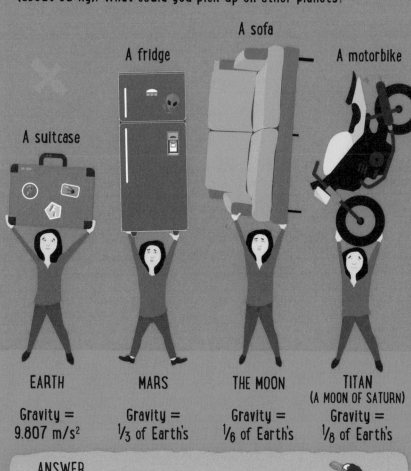

A sofa

A fridge

A motorbike

A suitcase

EARTH	MARS	THE MOON	TITAN (A MOON OF SATURN)
Gravity = 9.807 m/s²	Gravity = ⅓ of Earth's	Gravity = ⅙ of Earth's	Gravity = ⅛ of Earth's

ANSWER
The Antarctica fact is false. It's seriously huge – bigger than Europe. And NO ONE lives there. Scientists and tourists visit for short periods. But there are no towns or villages.

m/s² = meters per second per second.

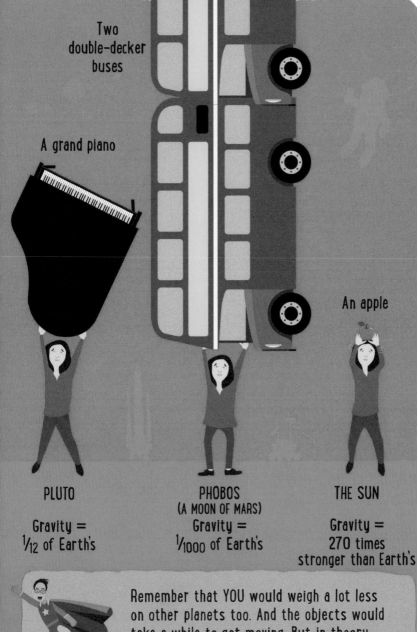

Two double-decker buses

A grand piano

An apple

PLUTO

Gravity = $\frac{1}{12}$ of Earth's

PHOBOS
(A MOON OF MARS)

Gravity = $\frac{1}{1000}$ of Earth's

THE SUN

Gravity = 270 times stronger than Earth's

Remember that YOU would weigh a lot less on other planets too. And the objects would take a while to get moving. But in theory, you could be a SUPERHERO in space.

MIGHTY METEORITES

On your way into space, you might pass a meteoroid hurtling in the opposite direction[*]. Sometimes these space rocks make it through the Earth's atmosphere. They're mostly harmless though...

Number of deaths in selected natural disasters

 KEY = 10,000 deaths

 Indian cyclone (1839)

300,000

 Yangtze River flood (1935)

145,000

 Eruption of Mount Tambora (1815)

92,000

 Avalanche in Peru (1950)

 **20,000**

 Every single meteor that has ever struck the Earth

ZERO recorded deaths

 According to the Natural History Museum, there have been no recorded deaths from meteorite strikes. Ever.

[*]A meteoroid becomes a meteor when it enters Earth's atmosphere and a meteorite when it lands on Earth.

Your chances of dying from a meteorite strike are very low.

Chances of dying from particular causes

Heart disease	23%	HIGH
Accidents	5%	
Meteorite	0.0001%	
Falling coconut	0.0000004%	
Shark attack	0.0000003%	LOW

There have been some close shaves though.

TOP THREE NEAR MISSES

In 1954, Ann Hodges from Alabama, USA, was fast asleep when a meteorite the size of a tennis ball broke through her ceiling, bounced off her radio and hit her on the thigh.

In 2003, Colby Navarro was working on his computer at home in Illinois, USA, when a meteorite fell through his house and broke his printer.

In 1992, Michelle Knapp from New York, USA, heard a crash outside her house. A meteorite the size of a football had squashed the boot of her car, shot straight through it and made a huge hole in her driveway.

In the past, meteorites have made some even **BIGGER** holes.

Vredfort – the biggest we know about – fell two billion years ago.

Kilimanjaro	Mount Everest	Vredfort meteorite
5.9 km	**8.8 km**	**15 km**

It hit the Earth at 22,000 mph and left a very big crater – **300 km** wide.

crater

That's **bigger** than Wales, UK

And about the same size as Iowa, USA

You can still see the remains of the crater in South Africa today.

WAY OUT WEATHER

You get some weird weather on other planets. But one of these is too strange to be true. Can you guess which one is made up?

DIAMOND HAILSTONES

On Neptune and Uranus, it rains diamonds. The high temperatures and pressures on these planets cause the jewels to form.

SQUARE SNOW

Instead of snowflakes, Mars has snow cubes. This snow is made of frozen carbon dioxide, rather than water.

FART FOG

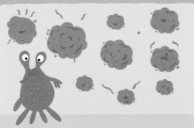

Venus is covered in sulphuric acid gas clouds, which makes everything smell of rotten eggs.

WILD WINDS

On Neptune, you'd constantly hear the boom of wind breaking the sound barrier. Its 1,500 mph winds could carry a hot-air balloon from London to Paris in 8.57 minutes.

FLOPPY RAIN

On Mercury, the rain is made of blue slime, so it's kind of sludgy. It falls slowly too – at less than one mph.

Which of these is unbelievable?

TOUGH CALL

Let's say you want to phone home from outer space. To do this, you'd use radio waves, which travel at about 300,000 km/sec. So your message could take a WHILE to get through.

MARS - 13-minute delay

PLUTO - 5-hour delay

ANSWER: There is no rain on Mercury. It doesn't have much of an atmosphere so there's hardly any weather at all.

ALPHA CENTAURI – 4.3-year delay
(nearest star to the Sun)

MEGREZ – 58-year delay
(part of the 'Big Dipper' constellation)

BETELGEUSE – 643-year delay
(part of the 'Orion' constellation)

BLUE PLANET

The Earth is the only planet in the solar system to have liquid water on its surface. In the past, it's had a lot of liquid water...

HISTORY OF SEA LEVEL CHANGE[*]

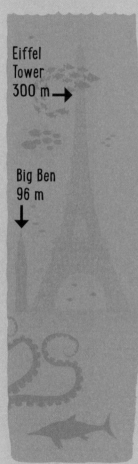

Eiffel Tower 300 m →

Big Ben 96 m ↓

440 MILLION YEARS AGO
400 m higher[**]

250 MILLION YEARS AGO
30 m lower

100 MILLION YEARS AGO
200 m higher

* Based on Hallam sea level curve.

UNDERWATER ROCKS!

Geologists don't always know exactly why the sea level rises and falls so dramatically, but it's usually linked to natural disasters and changing global temperatures.

50 MILLION YEARS AGO
100 m higher

200,000 YEARS AGO
130 m lower

SEA LEVELS
today

** Obviously the Eiffel Tower and Big Ben weren't there thousands of years ago. This is for 'demonstration purposes' only.

COSTING THE EARTH

Going to space can be expensive. But how much money are we talking?

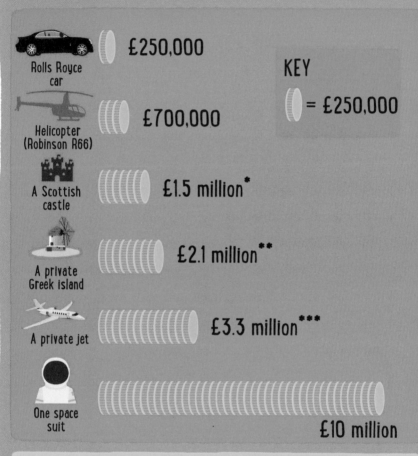

Rolls Royce car — £250,000

Helicopter (Robinson R66) — £700,000

A Scottish castle — £1.5 million*

A private Greek island — £2.1 million**

A private jet — £3.3 million***

One space suit — £10 million

KEY

= £250,000

WEAR AND TEAR
Each space suit on the International Space Station is used on average only 25 TIMES.

* The Craig in Angus, 2017 sale price.
** Nafsika Island, 2015 sale price.
*** Embraer Phenom 100E, 2016 sale price.

KEEP THE CHANGE

The average child in the UK gets £6.55 a week in pocket money.*
So it would take you 29,360 years to save up for a space suit.

SOARING COSTS

Each launch of the Saturn V rocket cost about £1 billion (in today's prices).

A lot of this cost was FUEL. Saturn V contained enough fuel to drive an average car around the world 800 times.

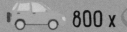 800 x

SKY-HIGH PRICES

The International Space Station is the most expensive structure ever built by humans.

 Palm Island, Dubai **£9 billion** (so far)

 Three Gorges Dam, China **£28 billion**

 International Space Station **£120 billion**

SUPPLY CHAIN

It also costs money to send material from Earth up to space station astronauts. Sending one single bottle of water costs up to £33,000 (in fuel and launch costs). Because of this, astronauts drink water recycled from their sweat and wee wherever possible. Yum!

Approximate transport costs

1 lemon
£7,300

 1 bottle of water
£33,000

 1 set of bagpipes
£200,000**

*2017 figures. Pocket money rates can go up as well as down.
**Taken into space in 2016 by astronaut Kjell Lindgren.

AND THE WINNER IS...

Welcome to the solar system's BEST PLANET awards. We've got SIX prizes to give out. But which of our heavenly bodies will win?

Average temperatures

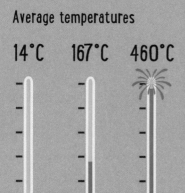

14°C   167°C   460°C

Earth   Mercury   Venus

HOTTEST PLANET

At an average temperature of 460°C, Venus can't be beat for heat. Standing on the surface would be like being in the hottest oven ever. In fact, you could cook a pizza in SEVEN SECONDS by just holding it out on your hand.

WINNER: VENUS

COLDEST PLANET

If Pluto was still considered a planet, then it would win this one, with an average temperature of -229°C. But alas in 2006, it was kicked out of the planet club, leaving the field clear for Neptune, with average temperatures of -214°C.

WINNER: NEPTUNE

Your freezer	Coldest ever temperature on Earth	Average temperature on Neptune	Average temperature on Pluto
- 14°C	- 89.2°C*	- 214°C*	- 229°C*

*In modern history.

Mercury

You are here

TINIEST PLANET

Not only is Mercury the smallest, it's also shrinking.
Since its formation 4.5 billion years ago, it's shrunk
by about 14 km and is still getting smaller.

PLANET WITH MOST MOONS

Jupiter has at least 67 moons.
The biggest (Ganymede) is larger
than Mercury. The smallest,
Jupiter LII, is about 2 km wide.
You could walk round the whole
of it in about ONE HOUR.

← Jupiter LII

WINNER: JUPITER

FLOATIEST PLANET

If you could find a bowl
of water big enough, Saturn
would float in it. That's because
it's basically a ball of hydrogen
and helium – the two lightest
elements in the universe.

WINNER: SATURN

300,000 kilometre-wide bowl

ONLY PLANET THAT WON'T KILL YOU IN MINUTES

There's not much competition for this one...

	EARTH	MERCURY	VENUS
Breathable air	✓	X	X
Pleasant temperatures	✓	X	X
Plenty of surface water	✓	X	X
Food growing everywhere	✓	X	X
A variety of animal life	✓	X	X
Solid ground to stand on (rather than gas)	✓	✓	✓
Atmospheric pressure that won't pull you apart	✓	X	X
Ozone layer protecting you from deadly radiation*	✓	X	X

*Venus and Mars have thin ozone layers that offer very little protection.

This is why astronomers tell us to LOOK AFTER EARTH. If we do set up colonies on other planets, all the evidence suggests that life there will be VERY difficult.

WINNER: EARTH

MARS	JUPITER	SATURN	URANUS	NEPTUNE
X	X	X	X	X
X	X	X	X	X
X	X	X	X	X
X	X	X	X	X
X	X	X	X	X
✓	X	X	X	X
X	X	X	X	X
X	X	X	X	X

STAYING POWER

The longest anyone has spent continuously in space is 437 days. How does that compare to other endurance records?

112 DAYS

The longest anyone has spent on a roller coaster is 112 DAYS. Richard Rodriguez rode the Pepsi Max Big One all day every day from May to September 2012.

In 1999, Bertrand Piccard and Brian Jones spent 19 DAYS and 22 HOURS in a hot-air balloon without landing once.

19 DAYS

11 DAYS

The longest anyone has gone without sleep is 11 DAYS and 24 MINUTES. Randy Gardner managed this in 1964.

REMEMBER: Endurance trials are difficult AND dangerous. Don't ever try them yourself.

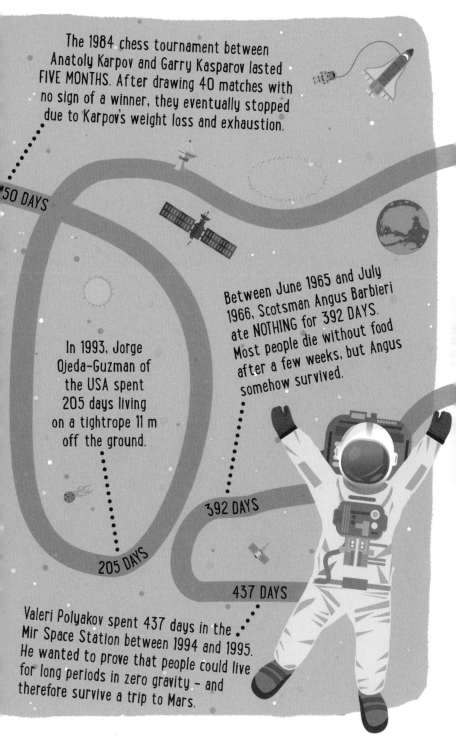

The 1984 chess tournament between Anatoly Karpov and Garry Kasparov lasted FIVE MONTHS. After drawing 40 matches with no sign of a winner, they eventually stopped due to Karpov's weight loss and exhaustion.

150 DAYS

Between June 1965 and July 1966, Scotsman Angus Barbieri ate NOTHING for 392 DAYS. Most people die without food after a few weeks, but Angus somehow survived.

In 1993, Jorge Ojeda-Guzman of the USA spent 205 days living on a tightrope 11 m off the ground.

392 DAYS

205 DAYS

437 DAYS

Valeri Polyakov spent 437 days in the Mir Space Station between 1994 and 1995. He wanted to prove that people could live for long periods in zero gravity – and therefore survive a trip to Mars.

STAR PERFORMERS

Our star – the Sun – is pretty big. But some stars are even bigger...

Our Sun – 864,000 miles in diameter.

Earth

If our Sun was as big as the Peony Nebula...

Earth a desert

Mercury swallowed up

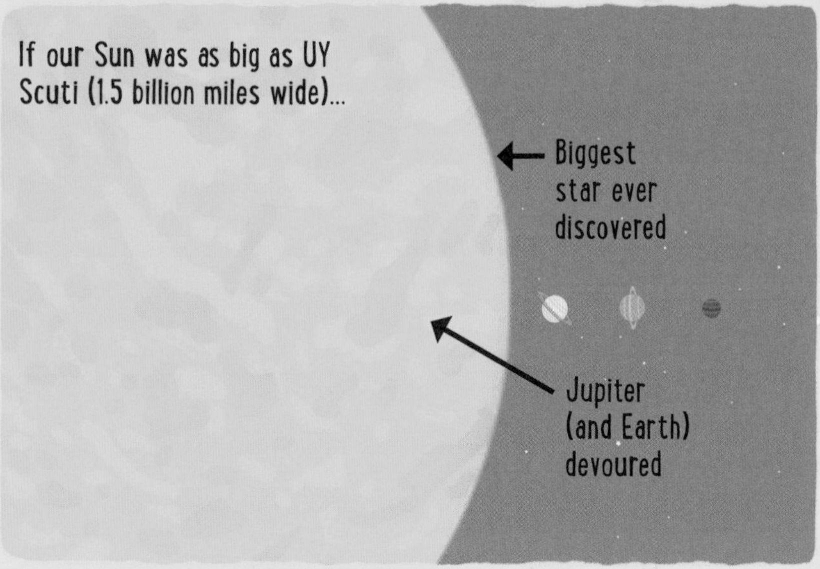

If our Sun was as big as UY Scuti (1.5 billion miles wide)...

← Biggest star ever discovered

Jupiter (and Earth) devoured

Or to put it another way...

If our Sun was the size of this dot:

 ← 1.5 mm wide

Peony Nebula would be the size of a grapefruit:

← 140 mm wide

And UY Scuti would be the size of a Zorb:

← 3 m wide

TAKE THAT!

The last large asteroid that hit the Earth wiped out the dinosaurs. Scientists have lots of plans to tackle the next one. But which of these wild ideas are REAL?

Paint it white.

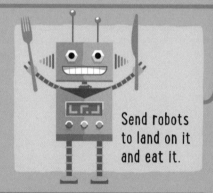

Send robots to land on it and eat it.

Place a solar-powered sail on top of it.

Catch it in a giant net and drag it to the Moon.

Let's hit the town!

Throw a giant bomb at it.

Surround it with giant mirrors.

TRUE
Space Works Engineering are planning to build a team of robot drillers that will eat into the rock and throw the debris into space.

FALSE
A bomb blast could create lots of smaller (equally deadly) asteroids. Plus gravity could simply squash the bits back together. Deflection is a better idea than destruction!

TRUE
In 2013, NASA announced a plan to catch an asteroid in a massive drawstring bag and then park it next to the Moon.

TRUE
Scientists believe that a solar sail would pick up energy from the Sun, speed the asteroid up and then it could be steered away from Earth.

TRUE
This could cause a fire on the rock's surface which – like a mini-rocket blaster – would push the asteroid in a different direction.

TRUE
White paint would reflect energy from the Sun, so the asteroid would radiate heat and subtly change its speed and direction.

YOU'VE GOT MAIL!

Arthur the Alien wants to send you a letter when he gets back home. In case you're wondering, here is your intergalactic address:

Your name
Your street
Your town
Your postcode
Your country
Earth
The Solar System
The Local Interstellar Arm
The Local Bubble
The Orion Arm
The Milky Way
The Local Group
The Virgo Cluster
The Virgo Supercluster
The Universe
The Multiverse

REMEMBER!

If you write a letter in space, normal pens won't work (because they rely on gravity to push the ink out). You could try an 'Anti-Gravity Space Pen' which uses gas to force the ink out and gel to stop the ink floating off (or you could use a pencil).

LISTEN UP!

Different planets have different atmospheres, which means that sound works very differently there.

How far would a scream travel in different places?

**EARTH
1 KM**

$((((((((((($ $)))))))))))$

**MARS
16 M**

$(($ $))$

**MOON
LESS THAN
1 CM***

$($ 🧍 $)$

**OUTER SPACE
0 CM**

🧍

Space is a vacuum which means there is no sound at all. A supernova could explode right next to you and you wouldn't hear a thing (it might hurt a bit though).

*You would probably detect faint vibrations of the person's agitation rather than the scream itself. The Moon has barely any atmosphere.

HEAD IN THE CLOUDS

Look at the clouds in the sky. Don't they seem light and fluffy? They're actually heavier than you think...

A one-kilometre³ cirrus cloud can weigh around 50 tonnes.

An average cumulus cloud can weigh 500 tonnes.

A storm cloud can weigh ONE MILLION tonnes.

In other words, a storm cloud can weigh the same as 24 ocean liners*.

SO HOW DO THEY FLOAT?

Although the water in a cloud weighs A LOT, it's spread across the cloud in *tiny* droplets. These droplets are also kept afloat by updrafts of warm air. However, eventually the clouds *do* stop floating. When the water droplets get too big, they fall to the ground, bit by bit, as rain.

KILLER CLOUDS

In 1959, William Rankin jumped out of his fighter jet when the engine failed. After his parachute opened, he drifted into a storm cloud, where he was thrown around by air currents, struck by lightning and hit by hailstones. A fall that should have taken a few minutes lasted for *40 minutes*. He finally landed in a forest – cold and bruised, but alive.

*The weight of an ocean liner is based on the Titanic (42,000 tonnes).

HERO OR ZERO?

If you travel in space, you'll spend most of it in zero gravity. But what's it like? One of the facts is false. See if you can guess which of these facts about life in zero gravity are true.

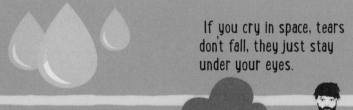

If you cry in space, tears don't fall, they just stay under your eyes.

You can move yourself (slowly) around the space station by farting.

If you're sick, it just floats around in front of your face.

You need to sleep by a fan or the carbon dioxide you breathe out can suffocate you.

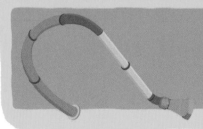

You have to effectively poo in a hoover. Otherwise the poo comes right back out.

Cutlery is attached to your food tray with magnets so it doesn't float around and stab you.

Most beds are on the wall (or ceiling). You have to strap yourself in at night. This includes strapping your head to the pillow or your head wobbles about!

Food has to be VERY spicy because your taste buds go numb. Astronaut Marsha Ivins recalls. 'I'd bring great chocolate with me and it would taste like wax.'

You can't have fizzy drinks because without gravity the bubbles don't float to the top. They stay exactly where they are.

Baths and showers are out because the water goes everywhere. You just have to wipe the dirt off.

Which fact is false? Answer over here.

PREHISTORIC PLANETS

If you'd flown through the solar system 200 million years ago – when dinosaurs walked the Earth – the planets would have looked a bit different.

Instead of seven continents, the Earth had just one – a huge supercontinent called Pangea.

The Moon was about 7,500 km closer to Earth (it moves 3.78 cm further away each year).

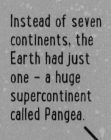

There were volcanoes erupting on Mars and the Moon. The Moon had active volcanoes until 50 million years ago.

ANSWER TO ZERO GRAVITY
You can't move around by farting. Although astronaut Chris Hadfield admitted, 'We all tried it. Too muffled. Not the right type of propulsive nozzle.'

There was no Orion. No Big Dipper. The Sun was three-quarters of the way round its orbit of the Milky Way so all the stars were in different places.

There was no famous Great Red Spot on Jupiter. The storm that causes the 'spot' probably only started a few hundred years ago.

Pluto probably didn't have any mountains yet – nor did it have a huge ice field on its surface.

Saturn was bald! According to some scientists, the planet's famous rings formed between 15 and 100 million years ago – so dinosaurs probably wouldn't have seen them.

This takes me back...

LIFE ON EARTH - PART TWO

Arthur the Alien has written down some facts about Earth's animals. But which one isn't quite right?

A roundworm is the most common animal. Four out of every five animals on Earth are roundworms. They live in oceans, forests, deserts, ice caps and inside people!

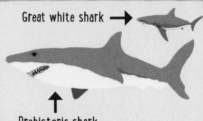

Great white shark ➡

⬆ Prehistoric shark

99.9% of all animal species that have ever lived on Earth are extinct (this means they have died out). Extinct animals include dinosaurs, dodos, giant kangaroos and 20-METRE-LONG sharks.

Koala		22 hours
Python		18 hours
Rabbit		11 hours
Elephant		3 hours
Ant	ZERO hours	

Most animals need sleep. A koala sleeps for most of the day. Ants 'rest' for short periods, but never sleep.

Animals need to defend themselves. A Texas horned lizard squirts blood out of its eyes. A sea cucumber shoots its intestines out of its bottom.

AVERAGE LIFESPAN

Mayfly = 1 day

Butterfly = 1 month

Mouse = 1 year

Giant tortoise = 100 years

Turritopsis dohrnii = Immortal

Some Earth creatures can live for a VERY long time. The Turritopsis dohrnii jellyfish can live forever (unless something eats it). After having babies, instead of dying, it changes back into a child again. And again.

NUMBER OF HEARTS

Hagfish 💜💜💜💜

Octopus 💜💜💜

Human 💜

Jellyfish NONE

Most animals have a heart. One is usually enough – but not always.

COLOUR OF BLOOD

Human   Octopus   Beetle

Leech   Marine worm   Spider (see-through blood)

Blood isn't always blood red. Especially if you're an invertebrate...

A goose poos every 12 minutes. A sloth poos once a week.

Vision can vary. An eagle has incredible eyesight. It can see a rabbit moving on the ground from 200 miles away. Bats, on the other hand, are completely blind.

Which animal fact sounds fishy to you? Turn the page to find the answer.

ROCKY ROAD

The lunar rover was designed to help astronauts explore the Moon. It meant they could go further and faster in their exploration than ever before.

How far did astronauts get from their landing craft?

BEFORE THE ROVER

Apollo 11
(July 1969)

60 m

The first men on the Moon

Apollo 12
(Nov 1969)

450 m

Apollo 14
(Jan 1971)

1.8 km

AFTER THE ROVER

Apollo 15
(July 1971)

5 km

Apollo 16
(April 1972)

4.5 km

Apollo 17
(Dec 1972)

7 km

ANSWER: Eagles have great vision but can only see for about two miles rather than 200! And bats aren't blind. All bats can see a little and some fruit bats can see three times further than YOU!

The rover weighed 218 kg on Earth but only about 36 kg on the moon (that's the weight of an average 11-year-old). If you want to know why, turn back to WEIGHT OFF MY MIND.

Driving a car on the Moon sounds cool, right? But could you pass a lunar rover driving test?

FAIL LUNAR ROVER DRIVING TEST

YOU DROVE MORE THAN TEN KM FROM THE LANDING MODULE
This is bad because you only have enough oxygen to survive a ten-kilometre walk back to your spacecraft if the rover breaks down.

YOU DROVE WITH THE SUN BEHIND YOU
Bad idea. This means all the shadows vanish. You can't see the rocks – everything is bright grey. You're heading for a crater!

YOU DROVE UP A STEEP HILL
Uh-oh. That rover's going over. A gentle hill of up to 25 degrees is OK. After that, it's a slippery slope.

DID YOU KNOW?
No woman has ever walked on the Moon. All 12 moon visitors were men. Fortunately, times have changed and by 2016, half of NASA's new astronaut class were women.

COLOSSAL COMETS

In 2000, scientists detected a comet with a 570-million-kilometre gas tail – the longest ever. But how long are we talking?

Distance from the Sun to the Earth — 150 million km

Comet ISON — 16 million km

Halley's Comet[*] — 100 million km

Great Comet of 1843 — 250 million km

Comet Hyakutake (longest tail ever)[**] — 570 million km

Going in the fastest ever manned spacecraft (25,000 mph), it would take you nearly TWO years to reach the end of Comet Hyakutake's tail.

Halley's comet is the Earth's most famous comet, passing overhead every 75 years. It last appeared in 1986 and will be back in 2061. How old will you be?

[*]1910 measurement of Halley's Comet. [**] The Great Comet of 2007 (Comet McNaught) might have had an even LONGER tail, but it was never officially measured.

DOWN TO EARTH

Ever felt strange after a plane flight? Well, a long SPACE flight can make your body feel even stranger.

Astronauts returning to Earth can find these things tricky:

WALKING
After spending months floating, astronauts often have trouble walking on Earth. 'It's like some evil giant is trying to press me into the ground,' said astronaut Samantha Cristoforetti in 2015.

FIGHTING OFF BUGS
In space, an astronaut's immune system goes haywire and this can cause health problems afterwards. Astronaut Andre Kuipers said, 'Back on Earth, I felt 100 years old for a few months.'

TALKING
Returning astronauts aren't used to the weight of their lips and tongue, so they often can't talk properly.

SEEING THINGS
Spending time in space can cause your eyeballs to get squeezed. This can make everything look blurry when you're back on Earth.

LIFTING AND CARRYING
Your bones and muscles shrink in zero gravity because you don't use them as much. So, back on Earth, even turning your neck can be difficult.

Most astronauts get back to normal in a month or two.

DIZZY HEIGHTS

Gravity on other planets is different than on Earth. So how high could WORLD RECORD high jumper Javier Sotomayor jump on other planets?

SOFT LANDING?
On other planets, Javier would land with the same force as if he'd jumped on Earth. So he might need a crash mat, but he wouldn't go SPLAT!

He could jump over a brachiosaurus.

He could jump over a giraffe.

He could jump over a house.

His world record high jump.

EARTH	MARS	MERCURY	MOON
2.45 m	6 m	6 m	14 m

For more on how gravity affects how heavy things are on different planets, see 'WEIGHT OFF MY MIND' earlier in the book.

He could jump over a skyscraper.

He could jump over a mountain. We'd need 60 extra pages to show the top of the mountain. (And his jump would take him over an hour too.)

He could jump over the Sphinx.

TITAN
(a moon of Saturn)
20 m

PLUTO
41 m

PHOBOS
(a moon of Mars)
2.5 km

REMEMBER: No one has actually TESTED jumping on any other planet — only the Moon. So we don't know for SURE what other factors might mess with Javier's jump...

ALIEN ATTACK!

Some people say they've spotted aliens like Arthur vising Earth...

There have been 110,265 reported sightings of aliens since 1905.*

KEY

1 alien
=
1,000
sightings

*As of 30th April 2017, Source: National UFO Reporting Centre.

The number of sightings has risen dramatically in the last 20 years.

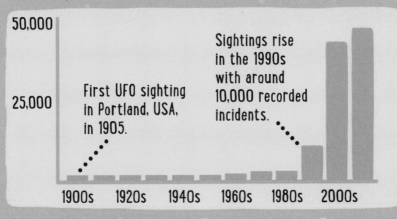

50,000

25,000

First UFO sighting in Portland, USA, in 1905.

Sightings rise in the 1990s with around 10,000 recorded incidents.

1900s   1920s   1940s   1960s   1980s   2000s

Aliens are most commonly spotted in the United States.**

USA   92.5%

Everywhere   7.5%
else

JULY

The most likely day to see aliens is the 4th of July where there are often over 1,000 sightings. The 4th of July is a national holiday in the USA. Lots of fireworks are set off which might explain why more aliens are 'seen.'

**This is partly because the National UFO Reporting Centre is based in the USA.

ALIEN SIGHTINGS

Here are three of the most famous alien sightings.

Rendlesham Forest Lights, UK

In 1980, a group of soldiers saw a series of mysterious lights in a forest near their military base in the UK. On entering the forest, they saw a glowing metal object, surrounded by lights. When they got closer, it moved off through the trees. Later that morning, they found triangular-shaped prints in the soil.

Roswell, USA

In 1947, it is claimed that an alien craft crash-landed in Roswell, USA, and that the government kept it a secret. UFO believers say there were dead bodies inside the UFO and the military may still have these bodies hidden away somewhere.

Portsmouth, USA

In 1961, Barney and Betty Hill claimed that they were kidnapped by aliens. They said a flying saucer had chased them in their car and beamed them up into their spaceship. When they were returned to Earth, their clothes were torn and both their watches had stopped.

There is no solid evidence that any of these events are linked to aliens. The flashing lights or spaceships are probably meteorites, lighthouses or aeroplanes. Alien kidnappings could be dreams or made-up stories. What do you think?

LET'S PARTY!

A year is how long it takes a planet to go round the Sun once. Planets orbit at different speeds, so you'd have fewer birthdays in some places.

← **1000 days*** →

MERCURY
A birthday every 88 days.

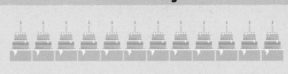

VENUS
A birthday every 225 days.

EARTH
A birthday every 365 ¼ days.

MARS
A birthday every 687 days.

NEPTUNE
A birthday every 165 Earth years.

If you were born on Neptune, you'd spend your whole life being ZERO. You'd also be the same age as your parents. And your grandparents.

*By days, we mean 'Earth days'.

STARING AT THE SUN

If you asked different people throughout history to explain what the Sun is, you'd get VERY different answers.

ANCIENT EGYPT

A giant dung beetle called Khepri rolls the Sun across the sky like a ball of poo, pushes it into the underworld at sunset and digs it up again in the east at dawn.

ANCIENT CHINA

There were originally ten suns which were supposed to shine one at a time. However, one day all ten came out and shone at once, scorching the Earth. A hero called Hou Yi shot nine down with a bow and arrow. Now there's just one.

AZTEC EMPIRE

There have been four suns before this one. This one is called Tonatiuh. If we don't offer him human sacrifices, he will refuse to move through the sky and all our crops will die.

TODAY

It's a giant ball of hydrogen and helium kept in place by gravity. It was created 4.6 billion years ago when a cloud of gas and dust got squashed together. Its surface temperature is over 5,000°C!

SIDE BY SIDE

Did you know that you could fit all the planets in the solar system between Earth and the Moon?

Earth →

The Moon →

THE MATHS
The Moon is about 398,000 km away from Earth (when it's at the furthest point in its orbit). All the planets' average diameters add up to 380,016 km. It all adds up!

So how far apart are the planets normally?

$X = C^2$
x 3 –
2c x 1
53 x1

THAT'S ABOUT THE SIZE OF IT

To give you a sense of cosmic distances, let's imagine the solar system is the size of a football pitch...

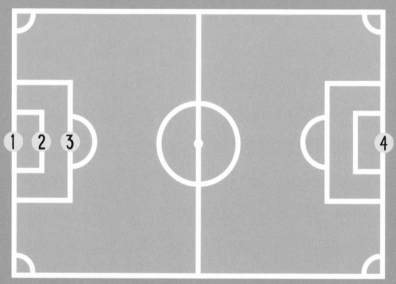

1 The Sun would be about the size of a ping pong ball, sitting on the goal line.

2 Earth would be a speck, less than one millimetre wide, three metres from the ping pong ball.

3 Jupiter, the largest planet, would be just on the edge of the penalty box, a tiny three-millimetre-wide gas ball.

4 Neptune is on the other goal line, a one-millimetre dot.

If the stadium were in London, UK, then the nearest stars (Alpha Centauri A and B) would be like a ping pong ball and a golf ball, sitting in the middle of Berlin, Germany – about 900 km away.

SUPER VOLCANO

Jupiter's moon, Io, has some of the
biggest volcanoes in the solar system.
Here's how high the plumes can reach.

480 km

400 km

322 km

235 km

100 km
where outer space
starts (on Earth)

70 km

13 km

Highest
clouds on
Earth

Tallest
volcano plume
recorded on
Earth (Taupo
eruption, 186 AD)

Skylab
space
station

Distance
reached by
Yuri Gagarin
(1961)*

International
Space
Station

Volcano
on Io

*The first man in space.

THE GREAT ESCAPE

If your rocket isn't going fast enough, it will be pulled back to the ground by gravity. So how fast do you need to go to escape different planets?

ESCAPE VELOCITY
This is minimum speed you need to be going to escape from the gravitational pull of a massive object in space.

EARTH	THE MOON	SATURN	URANUS
25,000 mph	5,300 mph	81,000 mph	48,000 mph

The fastest manned rocket we've ever built reached 25,000 mph. So we'd need even MORE powerful rockets if we wanted to take off from Saturn or Jupiter!

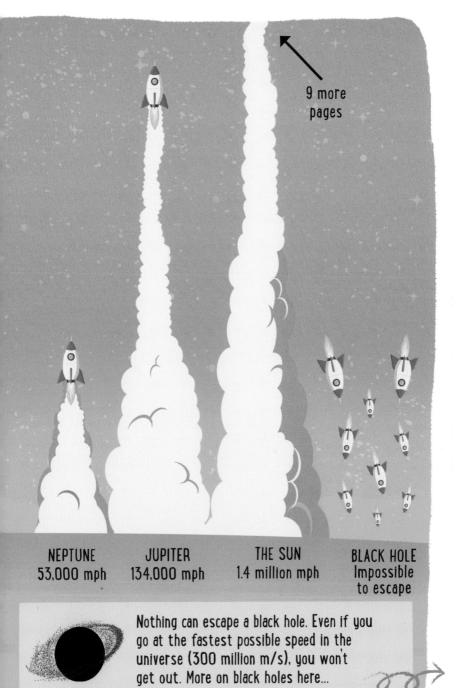

9 more pages

NEPTUNE
53,000 mph

JUPITER
134,000 mph

THE SUN
1.4 million mph

BLACK HOLE
Impossible
to escape

Nothing can escape a black hole. Even if you go at the fastest possible speed in the universe (300 million m/s), you won't get out. More on black holes here...

THE HOLE TRUTH

What happens if you fall into a black hole?

OK, so you've crossed the event horizon of a black hole.

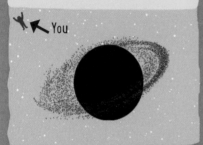

An event horizon is a black hole's point of no return. If you cross it, you're getting pulled in.

Uh-oh!

When you enter the black hole, the gravity pulling your toes...

I've put my foot in it.

...is stronger than the gravity pulling your head.

So you'd basically get turned into a huge string of spaghetti.

Now things get really weird. For you, this process would take a split second.

At the same time, you'd see the universe outside the black hole moving incredibly quickly.

If a friend was watching you from his spaceship, you'd see him get old...

...you'd watch his spaceship fall apart and vanish.

You'd potentially see thousands of years into the future...

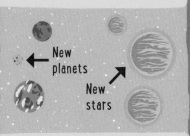

New planets

New stars

...all in a split second.

At the same time, your friend would see you being stretched incredibly slowly.

In fact, you'd probably look like you were frozen in time...

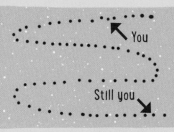

You

Still you

...stretched into a long string of atoms.

Sounds horrible? Well, unless you fancy a 17 QUADRILLION mile journey (2,800 light years) to our nearest black hole, you're unlikely to run (or fall) into one.

I'm in a dark place.

IN YOUR ELEMENT

Your body contains all kinds of precious metals.

The average human contains:

4.2 g of IRON

Enough to make a
ten-centimetre nail.

95 g of CHLORINE

Enough to disinfect
five swimming pools.

16 kg of CARBON

x 100
Enough to make
900 pencils.

780 g of PHOSPHORUS

Enough to make
2,200 matches.

Your body also contains:

| 120 mg of lead | 72 mg of copper | 2 mg of silver | 0.2 mg of gold |

If you could somehow remove the elements in your body and sell
them, you could make about £120 (or $150).

Now here's the weirdest part. All of these elements come from OUTER SPACE.

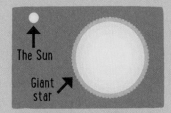

STEP 1:
In the middle of giant stars, temperatures rise to 10,000,000°C. This creates elements like carbon.

STEP 2:
When the star dies, its core gets squashed by its own gravity, resulting in a supernova. This creates heavy elements like iron and nickel.

Brighter than one billion suns

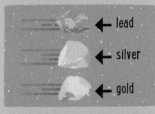

STEP 3:
The supernova explosion flings these elements across the universe.

← lead

← silver

← gold

STEP 4:
This stardust gets clumped together to form new stars and planets – like Earth.

STEP 5:
Over time, these elements combine and slowly turn into rocks, plants, animals... and YOU!

In other words, everything in your body originally comes from STARS.

HERE BE MONSTERS!

You might not think too much about the Sun and the Moon. But if you're a monster, it can be a matter of life and death.

JANUARY FEBRUARY MARCH APRIL MAY JUNE

JULY AUGUST SEPTEMBER OCTOBER NOVEMBER DECEMBER

There is a full moon every 30 days. So if you're a werewolf, there are 12 TIMES a year when you have to watch ow-ow-owt!

If you were a Mad Scientist making a Frankenstein's monster, you could bring 100 of them to life every second. Why? Because, every second, 100 lightning bolts hit Earth, carrying up to ONE BILLION volts of electricity each.

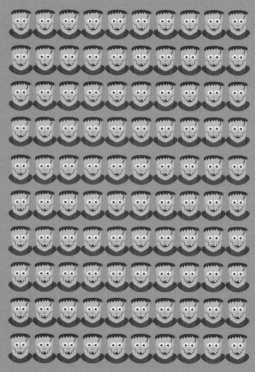

If you were a vampire, then sunlight would kill you. So where in the universe would you find guaranteed DARKNESS?

1. THE NORTH AND SOUTH POLES

The North Pole is in total darkness from September to March. The South Pole is in darkness from March to September. So as long as you fly from one to the other every six months, then you'll be in continuous NIGHT.

Got to fly.

Show off.

WHAT THE SUN LOOKS LIKE ON DIFFERENT PLANETS

Mercury   Earth Neptune

2. NEPTUNE

Neptune is the darkest planet in the solar system. The sun is 900 times dimmer than it is on Earth. So even during the day, your sensitive skin should be safe.

3. PROXIMA CENTAURI B

This is probably the best place. It's an Earth-like planet 4.2 light years away. Scientists believe that it's tidally locked to its sun which means that one-half of it is *always* in blazing sunshine and the other half is *always* pitch black and ice cold. Vampire paradise!

COSMIC CREATURES

All of these animals have been to space except one. Can you guess which creature has never left Planet Earth?

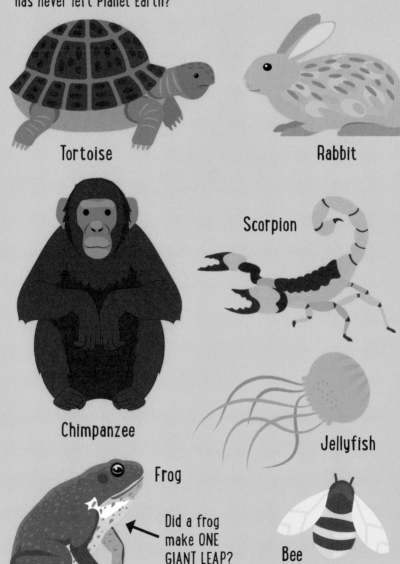

Tortoise

Rabbit

Scorpion

Chimpanzee

Jellyfish

Frog

Did a frog make ONE GIANT LEAP?

Bee

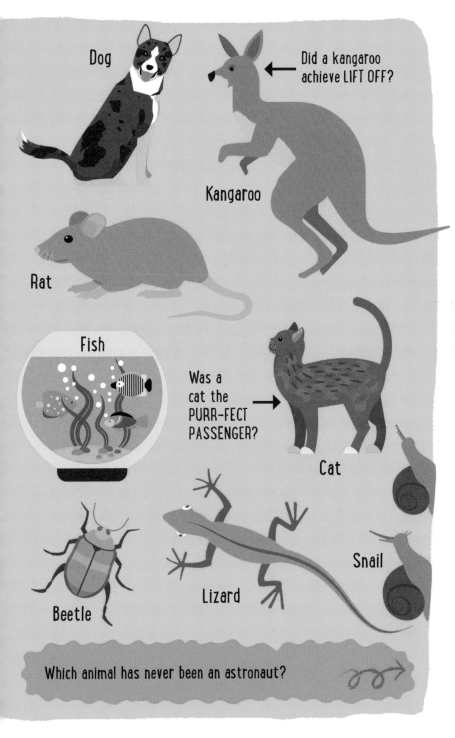

CRUNCH TIME!

There have been some huge CRASH LANDINGS in space history. And guess what – most of them were DELIBERATE. But why?

In 2009, NASA wanted to see if there was water on the Moon. So they purposely crashed a spacecraft into the Moon's south pole. This sent up a huge plume of vapour, which another spacecraft analysed – and found water!

In 2015, a $446 million spacecraft was deliberately smashed into Mercury at 8,750 mph, creating a 15-metre crater. The spacecraft had run out of fuel and, this way, at least scientists could study the crater that was left behind.

Answer
A kangaroo has never been on a space vacation. Which is a shame because imagine how high it could bounce in zero gravity!

In 2003, the probe Galileo was deliberately flown into Jupiter at 108,000 mph. This was to avoid it crashing into Jupiter's moon, Europa, which may have life on it. Galileo didn't exactly CRASH because Jupiter is made of gas. Instead it survived for 78 minutes INSIDE Jupiter before being SQUISHED.

In 2016, the Rosetta probe was purposely crashed into a four-kilometre-wide comet. The probe had been studying the comet for two years, and crashing it meant that scientists got INCREDIBLE close-up photos of the comet's surface.

In 2012, two probes, Ebb and Flow, were sent into a deliberate 'death plunge' into the far side of the Moon. This was to avoid them crashing into any of the Moon's historical sites – like Neil Armstrong's footprints or the three lunar rovers.

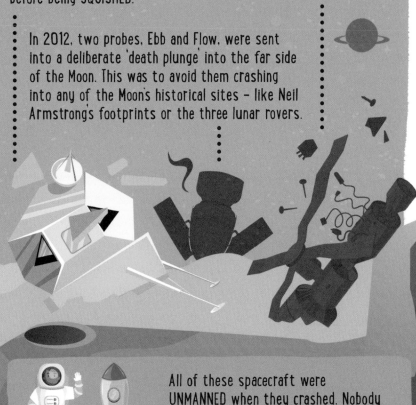

All of these spacecraft were UNMANNED when they crashed. Nobody would ever deliberately crash a rocket with people (or animals) on board!

A DAY IN THE LIFE

If the Earth's 4.6 billion-year history were squashed into 24 hours, here's what a day would look like:

MIDNIGHT

12:00 AM: Earth is formed by a swirling cloud of gas and dust. Half an hour later, the Earth is hit by a giant rock and the Moon is formed.

3 AM

4:10 AM: Water in the atmosphere turns into rain, creating the oceans. About a minute later, very simple bacteria-like organisms appear – and life on Earth begins.

6 AM

6:00 AM: Life is still tiny single-celled organisms and will be for another 14 hours. But given that Earth is lashed by hurricanes and the sea is boiling hot, it's probably for the best.

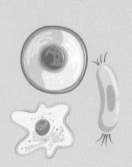

9 AM

NOON

11:28 AM: Lots of oxygen gets released into the atmosphere. This will come in handy for plants and animals in about ten hours' time.

NOON

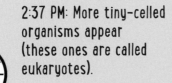

3 PM

2:37 PM: More tiny-celled organisms appear (these ones are called eukaryotes).

You look... different.

5:44 PM: Red and brown algae appear. Life is about to get... complicated.

6 PM

8:11 PM: The first jellyfish appear.

9 PM

9:20 PM: The first fish swim into view, followed by the first shark (30 minutes later).

9:47 PM: The first trees start to grow.

10:48 PM: The dinosaurs rock up.

11:39 PM: The dinosaurs are wiped out (probably) by an asteroid.

MIDNIGHT

Let's go out clubbing!

At THREE SECONDS to midnight, the first humans appear.

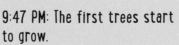

SPACE PIZZA

There's always 'space' for another slice.

In 2001, Pizza Hut delivered a six-inch pizza to Yuri Usachov on the International Space Station (ISS).

Typical distance	Distance to the ISS

5 km	300 km

It took Pizza Hut a year to make, test and deliver the pizza.

Typical delivery time	Delivery to the ISS
	2000–2001
30 mins	One year

Yuri didn't have to pay the delivery guy a SINGLE PENNY. In fact, Pizza Hut paid Yuri and the Russian Space Agency $1 million instead!

Average takeaway pizza cost (2017)

From a restaurant	£10
From a supermarket	£2.50
For Yuri Usachov	FREE

In 2011, Domino's Pizza considered building a pizza restaurant on the MOON. They worked out it would cost £13.4 billion to transport building materials and pizza ovens to the Moon in 15 rockets.

If Americans did colonise the Moon, Domino's Pizza could have a lot of customers. Americans eat 100 acres of pizza a day.

x 62

That's about 62 football (or soccer) pitches.

ROLL WITH IT!

When the Earth first formed 4.6 billion years ago, it spun a lot faster so one day was a lot shorter. The days have been getting longer ever since.

KEY
● = 1 DAY

4.5 BILLION YEARS AGO	1 DAY = ●●●	2.5 HOURS LONG*
3.5 BILLION YEARS	1 DAY = ●●●●●●●●●●●	12 HOURS LONG
620 MILLION YEARS	1 DAY = ●●●●●●●●●●●●●●●●●●●●●	22 HOURS LONG
TODAY	1 DAY = ●●●●●●●●●●●●●●●●●●●●●●●	24 HOURS LONG
1 BILLION YEARS TIME	1 DAY = ●●●●●●●●●●●●●●●●●●●●●●●●●●●●	29 HOURS LONG (ROUGHLY)**

As the days get longer, our years get shorter. For example, 350 million years ago, although a day was 23 hours, a YEAR was 385 days.

The Earth is slowing down because of our old friend the Moon. But this is a GOOD THING. Before the Moon arrived, the Earth spun so fast, NO LIFE was possible. It was like being in a giant blender full of magma.

*Some scientists believe it was more like five hours.
** No one REALLY knows for sure what Earth will be like in one billion years...

SUPER SCIENCE FICTION

Some of the most popular films are set in space. How many of these blockbusters have you seen?

Most successful science fiction films (money made in US dollars*):

Star Wars: A New Hope (1977) $1.6 billion

E.T. The Extra-Terrestrial (1982) $1.3 billion

Star Wars: The Force Awakens (2015) $961 million

The Empire Strikes Back (1980) $873 million

Avatar (2009) $865 million

Return of the Jedi (1983) $836 million

Star Wars: The Phantom Menace (1999) $803 million

The Avengers (2012) $683 million

Rogue One: A Star Wars Story (2016) $537 million

Star Wars: Revenge of the Sith (2005) $527 million

KEY

$ = $100 million

JUST OUTSIDE THE TOP 10

Superman, Close Encounters of the Third Kind, Men in Black.

*All the box office numbers have been converted to today's prices. This is because prices have gone up (for example, in 1974 a cinema ticket in the UK was 45p, now it's over £10).

Films can also cost a lot to make.

Total movie budget:

THE FORCE AWAKENS (2015)
$306 MILLION
(£240 MILLION)

ROGUE ONE (2016)
$265 MILLION
(£204 MILLION)

WALL-E (2008)
$180 MILLION
(£140 MILLION)

ONE CHILD

ONE ADULT

The cost of the Indian Mars mission was £43.8 million. Making *The Force Awakens* cost almost SIX TIMES more than actually going into space.

In 2016, British film fans were asked to name their favourite TV and film aliens. Is your favourite on the list?*

1. The Doctor *(Doctor Who)*
2. Darth Vader *(Star Wars)*
3. Han Solo *(Star Wars)*
4. Mr Spock *(Star Trek)*
5. Captain Jack Harkness *(Doctor Who / Torchwood)*

JUST OUTSIDE THE TOP 5:

James T Kirk *(Star Trek)*
Captain Jean-Luc Picard *(Star Trek: The Next Generation)*

*Based on a 2016 BFI poll. TV shows and films with a 15 certificate or above have been omitted from our list.

MOVIE MISTAKES

Movies set in space often stretch the truth a bit. Here are six of the most common film fibs.

LOUD NOISES

In space movies, there are lots of engines roaring and rockets blasting. In reality, space is a vacuum. So there's no sound. Ever.

BIG EXPLOSIONS

There's no oxygen in space, so nothing can catch fire. When that spaceship 'explodes', there'd be no fireballs. It would just sort of... fall apart.

FLOATING DEBRIS

After something blows up in a movie, there are usually bits of spaceship hovering in mid-air. But in space, if something explodes, the debris doesn't stop moving unless it hits something. There's no air resistance. The junk could keep hurtling forwards FOREVER.

ASTEROID BELTS

What about ships having to steer round giant rocks in an asteroid belt? Looks IMPOSSIBLE, right? Well, in the asteroid belt in our solar system, the rocks are around 600,000 miles apart. In other asteroid belts, they're even further apart. You'd have to have rocks in your head to crash into one.

TALKING TO ALIENS ON DISTANT PLANETS

How about this scene? An alien leader appears on a ship's giant monitor demanding surrender. The human captain fires back an answer. In reality, there's a HUGE delay if you're talking in space. For example, it takes four hours to send a message from Earth to Neptune.

ASTRONAUTS THAT ARE THE WRONG SIZE

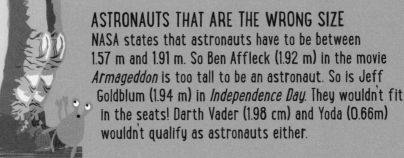

NASA states that astronauts have to be between 1.57 m and 1.91 m. So Ben Affleck (1.92 m) in the movie *Armageddon* is too tall to be an astronaut. So is Jeff Goldblum (1.94 m) in *Independence Day*. They wouldn't fit in the seats! Darth Vader (1.98 cm) and Yoda (0.66m) wouldn't qualify as astronauts either.

HUBBLE TROUBLE

The more you look, the more you see...

In 2003, the Hubble Space telescope was pointed at an empty square of sky.

Nothing interesting had ever been seen in this square before.

And nobody expected to find anything now.

The square was TINY too. About one tenth the size of the full Moon in the sky.

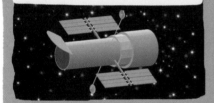

The square of nothingness

The Moon

The astronomers kept the telescope trained on the square for several months...

SEPT OCT NOV DEC

This meant that they could capture even the faintest light.

They got a surprise...

A picture of 10,000 galaxies.

Not stars. Not planets. GALAXIES. Each with millions of stars. EACH.

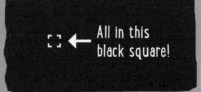 ← All in this black square!

So that's why scientists think there are about ten trillion galaxies and one septillion stars in the sky (that's one with 24 zeroes).

EXTREME EXOPLANETS

Before 1995, we didn't know for sure that there were planets outside our solar system. Now we've discovered thousands. But not many are worth a visit...

Kepler-16b: 196 light years away
This planet orbits two stars. So it has two suns in the sky.

Kepler-10b: 564 light years away
Fancy a dip? This whole planet is covered with hot lava oceans. It also enjoys one trillion lightning flashes an hour.

WASP-12b: 1,200 light years away
This planet has been stretched into an egg shape by the gravitational pull of its star. It hurtles around its sun in 1.1 days (Earth takes 365.2 days).

Kepler-1520b: 2,074 light years away
Scientists believe that the outer crust of this planet has been vaporised by its sun, leaving just an iron ball, rolling through space.

EARTH'S TWIN? LHS 1140b
Scientists have found over 50 planets so far that are around the same size and temperature as the Earth. However, LHS 1140b has been called a 'second Earth' because it may have an atmosphere like ours – which means there might be life on it!

You remind me of someone...

FIRE AND ICE

The universe can get awesomely hot.
And awesomely cold.

5.5 trillion°C
Hottest temperature ever created on Earth, by the Large Hadron Collider in Switzerland. It was only created for a split second by smashing two lead atoms into each other.

6,000°C
The temperature of the Sun's surface. Also the temperature of the Earth's core.

100 nonillion°C
The temperature of the Big Bang. That's one with 32 zeroes. The hottest it's ever been anywhere (probably).

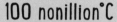

100 billion°C
The temperature of a blue supergiant star just before it explodes into a supernova.

AWESOMELY
HOT

INCREDIBLY
HOT

VERY
HOT

JUST RIGHT
The Earth's average temperature is around 14°C. And your average body temperature is 37°C.

Everything's cool.

-223°C
The temperature on the coldest planet in the universe (that we know about). Its name is OGLE-2005-BLG-390Lb. Catchy, right?

-153°C
The temperature on the 'dark side of the Moon' (the side that doesn't face the Earth).

-273°C
The coldest possible temperature, known as Absolute Zero. Scientists in Boston, USA, managed to cool a gas to one-billionth of a degree above Absolute Zero in 2003. And supermassive black holes almost get down to absolute zero — but not quite.

-270°C
The average temperature of the universe. And as the universe keeps expanding, it will get EVEN COLDER.

A BIT NIPPY   GETTING SERIOUSLY CHILLY   AWESOMELY COLD

ANIMAL SUPERSTARS

Constellations are often named after animals, although it's sometimes hard to work out why. Have a look at these star constellations and see if you can work out what their 'animal name' is.

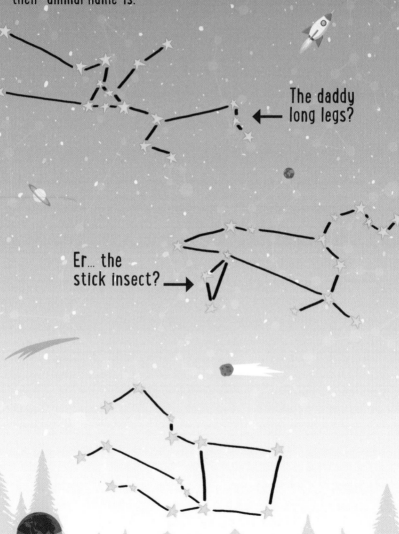

The daddy long legs?

Er... the stick insect?

NORTHERN HEMISPHERE STARS

These constellations are all named after one of these animals. Can you guess which is which?

1. Phoenix
2. Lion
3. Horse
4. Water snake
5. Bull
6. Fish
7. Toucan
8. Scorpion

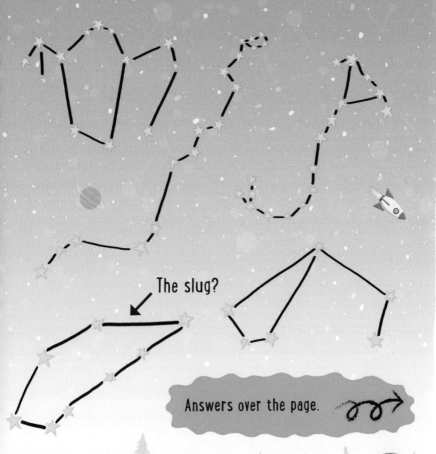

The slug?

Answers over the page.

SOUTHERN HEMISPHERE STARS

ANIMAL SUPERSTARS

Some of these were more obvious than others, right?
Can you think of BETTER names for these constellations?

THE BULL
(TAURUS)

THE LION
(LEO)

THE HORSE
(PEGASUS)

NORTHERN HEMISPHERE STARS

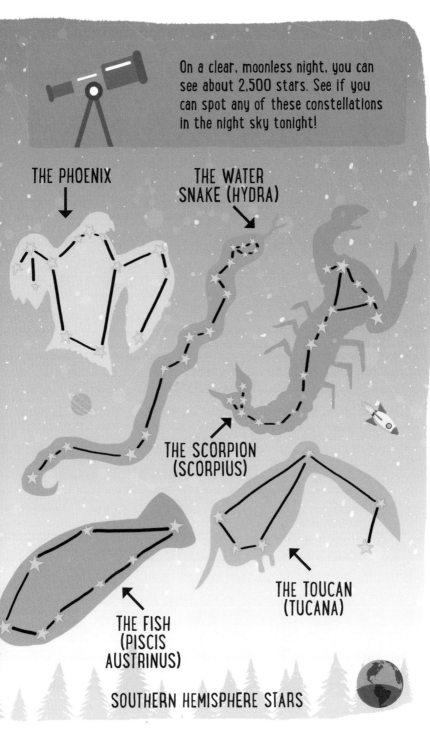

On a clear, moonless night, you can see about 2,500 stars. See if you can spot any of these constellations in the night sky tonight!

THE PHOENIX

THE WATER SNAKE (HYDRA)

THE SCORPION (SCORPIUS)

THE TOUCAN (TUCANA)

THE FISH (PISCIS AUSTRINUS)

SOUTHERN HEMISPHERE STARS

HEAVY GOING

A neutron star is the densest thing in the universe. And maybe the strangest.

WHAT IS A NEUTRON STAR?

It's what happens when a gigantic star dies in a supernova and its core collapses, squashing all its atoms together. They're sometimes known as 'zombies of the skies' because they keep shining even though they're dead and they eat any other stars that get too close.

HOW DENSE ARE WE TALKING?

One teaspoon of a neutron star would weigh the same as a mountain.

Neutron Star

Several billion tonnes

Several billion tonnes

AND IT GETS SCARIER...

x 50 TRILLION

If you could place that ONE TEASPOON on Earth, it would release *50 trillion* times the energy of the Hiroshima bomb of 1945, destroying all life on Earth.

100 TIMES STRONGER

However, you probably couldn't scoop up a teaspoon of a neutron star because its crust is 100 billion times stronger than steel. Your spoon would definitely break.

OUR SUN
6,000°C

NEUTRON STAR
1,000,000°C

Also, its gravity is 200 billion times more powerful than the Earth's, which would rapidly turn you into the universe's flattest pancake.

Plus you couldn't get close to a neutron star because its average temperature is around 1,000,000°C.

EARTH
1 G

ROLLER COASTER
6 G

NEUTRON STAR
200 BILLION G

DIAMETER OF SELECTED PLANETS

JUPITER
139,822 KM
WIDE

EARTH
12,742 KM
WIDE

↑
MOON
3,474 KM
WIDE

↑
PLUTO
2,370 KM
WIDE

↑
NEUTRON STAR
20 KM
WIDE

Fortunately, neutron stars are TINY in space terms – about 20 km wide. So even though there are thought to be 100 million 'zombie stars' hiding away in the Milky Way, you'd be DEAD unlucky to get eaten by one...

SPACE TALK

The scientists that study space like to keep things very simple.
So space concepts usually have very obvious names.

Q: What is the name for the big explosion that created the entire universe?
A: The Big Bang.

Q: What's the name of that giant telescope they built in Chile?
A: The Very Large Telescope (or VLT).

Q: What are they calling the even bigger one that they started to build?
A: The Extremely Large Telescope (or ELT).

Q: What are those big black holes in space called?
A: Black holes.

Q: What are the really HUGE black holes called?
A: Supermassive black holes.

Q: You know that big red spot on Jupiter? What's that called?
A: The Great Red Spot.

Q: And you know the dark energy that is making the universe expand? I bet that's got a really long and complicated name. Like, astro-quantum nano-electrons.
A: That dark energy is called... dark energy.

See? Scientific language doesn't have to make your brain hurt.

SPEED OF SPIN

How fast do planets in the solar system spin?

MERCURY   1 DAY = 59 DAYS
Mercury spins on its axis REALLY slowly – about
6.7 mph. (You can probably RUN faster than that!)

EARTH   1 DAY = 24 HOURS
Earth spins at about 1,037 mph. This means, even
if you stand still, you move over 20,000 miles
each day!

JUPITER   1 DAY = 10 HOURS
Jupiter is pretty fast for a big planet! It spins
round at almost 30,000 mph. Because it's made of
gas, its equator swirls round faster than its poles.

HAUMEA   1 DAY = 4 HOURS
This dwarf planet spins so fast that it has been
STRETCHED into a rugby ball shape. If it spun much
faster, it would fly apart completely.

Venus is strange for two reasons. Firstly,
it spins the OTHER way. Secondly, it spins
UNBELIEVABLY slowly (4 mph). It takes
243 DAYS to spin round once. In fact, one
day is longer than one year (224 days).
Both daytime and night-time last for MONTHS.

LIFE ON EARTH – PART 3

For Arthur the Alien's last dispatch, he's looking at Earth's geography. But which fact has he got upside down? (That's a clue!)

Although it's called Earth, ... most of Earth is water – 71% of its surface is covered by oceans, lakes and ice caps.

There are about .... three trillion trees on Earth. That's around 400 trees for every human being.

The worst volcano eruption in modern history was probably Indonesia's Mount Tambora. It erupted in 1815, blocking out the sun for months and causing the Earth's temperature to drop by 3°C.

The driest place on Earth is probably the Dry Valleys area of Antarctica, which is believed to have had no rainfall for over two million years.

Russia is the largest country in the world. You could fit the UK into Russia 67 times. It's almost twice as big as the USA.

Can you spot Arthur's mistake?

Almost 5,000 people have climbed Mount Everest, the world's highest mountain. In 2014, Wim Hof successfully climbed Everest wearing only shorts. In 2009, Jordan Romero climbed it when he was 13 making him the youngest person ever to do so.

The continent of Asia is bigger than the Moon. It is over 17 million square miles (the Moon's surface is 14.6 million square miles).

Almost all of the land on Earth has been visited by humans, but less than 5% of the ocean has been explored.

If you are in the northern half of the planet (e.g. the US or Europe), bathwater swirls anti-clockwise as it drains away. If you are in the southern half (e.g. Australia), then bathwater swirls clockwise.

Answer over here.

RADIO SILENCE

Sorry to spoil everyone's fun, but we might never talk to any aliens like Arthur, even if they exist... Here's why.

Problem 1: The aliens will need to be as smart as (or smarter than) us.

There are about 8.7 million species on Earth. So far, only one of these species (us) has developed the technology to talk to alien planets.

Problem 2: The aliens will need to have developed a civilized society.

Humans have been around for about 200,000 years. For most of that time, we ran around with big sticks, trying to kill each other.

Problem 3: The aliens need to have discovered the RIGHT technology.

The best way we've discovered of communicating over huge distances is radio waves. Which we only discovered about 120 years ago.

ANSWER: No, bathwater doesn't swirl different ways in different places. This myth is based on the Coriolis effect, which means that hurricanes in the northern hemisphere tend to rotate anti-clockwise and hurricanes south of the equator tend to rotate clockwise. You'd need a GIANT bath for this to affect your bathwater!

Problem 4: The aliens have to WANT to be found.

Even though we discovered radio waves over a century ago, we've only been trying to communicate with other planets since the 1970s.

Problem 5: The aliens and us need to exist at the right moment in our planets' histories.

The Earth has been here for over four billion years. For most of that time, it had no life on it, or it was covered in bacteria.

They invited us over in 2099.

Problem 6: Would a useful conversation be possible?

The nearest Earth-like planets are trillions of miles away and it would take YEARS for them to receive a message from us and then YEARS for us to hear their reply.

Problem 7: Would we understand a word the aliens are saying?

BURBLE
SPLOOT
TEASMAID
PARSNIP
WIGWAM

Love, Arthur x

There have been millions of human languages since we first evolved and there are over 7,000 right now. These include many different alphabets and some languages with no alphabet at all.

What do you think? Will we ever connect with our ALIEN FRIENDS? What would you say to them if we did make contact?

EARTH ROCKS!

What about exploring our own planet? What would happen if you drilled a hole through the middle of the Earth and jumped in?

Let's start by saying, for this to work, lots of incredible things would have to happen.

First you'd have to invent a machine that could drill through the Earth's mantle and crust.

Like the Koba Superdeep Borehole Drill.

The Koba drill managed to get 12 km down...

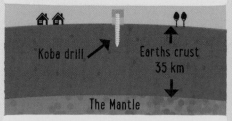

Koba drill

Earths crust 35 km

The Mantle

...that's 0.1% of the way.

Then it became too hot to drill any further.

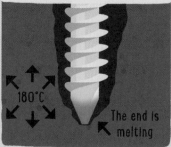

180°C

The end is melting

Next you'd have to invent a suit that would stop you being cooked alive.

Earth's core 6,000°C

Temperature of Sun 6,000°C

This magic suit would also have to stop you bouncing off the walls.

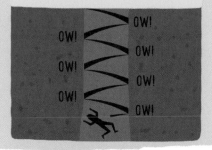

OW! OW! OW! OW! OW! OW! OW! OW! OW! OW!

Because of the Earth's rotation, you'd hit the sides constantly.

Rotation speed: 1,000 mph

PLUS air resistance would slow you down.

So by the time you got to the centre, you'd just stop and float.

BUT let's assume:

✓ The hole is a vacuum (with no air resistance).

✓ You build a heatproof suit.

✓ You enjoy bouncing off walls.

This is what would (probably) happen. You'd start falling fast.

22 mph
44 mph
66 mph
88 mph
110 mph

That was five seconds.

There'd be a loud boom as you broke the sound barrier.

767 mph

Boom!

Sorry!

When you got to the centre, you'd be at top speed.

18,000 mph

Half way there!

You'd be travelling so fast, you'd be carried across to the other side of the hole.

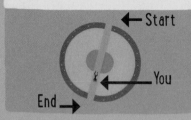

← Start

You

End →

You'd reach the other side of the Earth in 42 minutes.

Start   End

You'd rise up out of the hole, stop in mid-air for a few seconds...

Then you'd fall BACK into the hole.

You'd then continue to fall back and forth through the middle of the Earth.

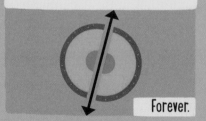

Forever.

Unless you ask a friend to grab you.

QUIZ
When William Hershel first discovered Uranus, what did he want to call it?
a) Uranus b) Zeus c) George   Answer over there...

NAMING NAMES

If you discover a new asteroid or minor planet, you get to name it yourself! However there are some rules...

MINOR PLANET NAMING COMMITTEE

SUGGESTED NAME OF NEW PLANET	STATUS	REASON
Supercalifragilisticexpialidocious	REJECTED	Name must have fewer than 17 letters.
Zxkkqpxx	REJECTED	Name must be easy to pronounce.
Big Farty Poo Bum	REJECTED	Name must not contain RUDE words.
Squidgie	REJECTED	Must not be name of pet.
Mars	REJECTED	Name already taken.
Planet Awesome	ACCEPTED	New planet named!

What would you call a planet if you discovered it?
Here are some ACTUAL examples of minor planet names.

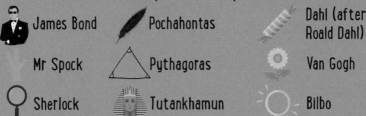

James Bond

Pochahontas

Dahl (after Roald Dahl)

Mr Spock

Pythagoras

Van Gogh

Sherlock

Tutankhamun

Bilbo

ANSWER: He wanted to call it George after King George III of England.

FEEL THE HEAT

The Sun is seriously hot...

It's 150 MILLION km away but you can't even LOOK at it for more than a few SECONDS without damaging your eyesight.

The sun's rays travel for EIGHT MINUTES across millions of miles to get here. But they can still burn your skin in less than 15 minutes on a hot day (so wear sunscreen!).

The Earth has an atmosphere that protects us. This means that only HALF of the Sun's energy reaches the Earth's surface. So the sun is around TWICE as hot as you think!

Remember too that the Sun gives off heat in ALL directions. The Earth gets less than one billionth of the Sun's total energy output. You could have thousands of Earths all around the Sun, and the Sun would happily heat all of them!

In one second, the Sun gives off more energy than has been used in the whole history of mankind.

And the Sun's energy can do amazing things...

The International Space Station has 2,500 m² of solar panels (almost half a football field).

The four sets of solar arrays can generate up to 120 kWh of electricity. That would power about 40 homes on Earth.

About 40% of the energy generated goes directly to the ISS to power their lights, computers and life-support systems.

The other 60% is stored in batteries. This ensures that the ISS still gets power during the 'eclipse' part of its orbit (when sunlight is blocked by the Earth). This lasts for 35 minutes of each 90-minute orbit.

A WASTE OF SPACE

Arthur's managed to get a spaceship working and is on his way home. The only problem is he has to steer through Earth's SPACE JUNK.

There are over 150 million pieces of space junk measuring one millimetre or more in length. They all whizz round at speeds of at least 17,500 mph.

Before 1957, there was no space junk. The first piece appeared when the Sputnik satellite was launched in 1957. It used a rocket to blast itself into space, then ditched this rocket once it had got high enough.

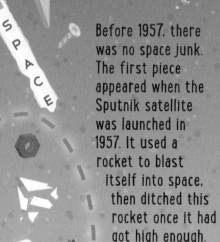

The biggest pieces of space junk tend to be old satellites, rocket parts and debris from crashes and collisions.

There's weird stuff up there too, including a toothbrush, a blanket and a camera. In 2008, Heide Stefanyshyn-Piper dropped a bag of tools during a spacewalk.

Small bits of space junk can be LETHAL because they travel at such high speeds. A tiny fleck of paint could kill an astronaut on a space walk. A paint fleck recently smashed into a window in the International Space Station (ISS), causing a nasty crack which they had to quickly repair.

A lot of space junk is caused by space junk smashing into other space junk and creating SMALLER pieces of space junk. In 2009, a US satellite collided with some space junk at 26,500 mph, creating thousands of new bits of trash.

There's more...

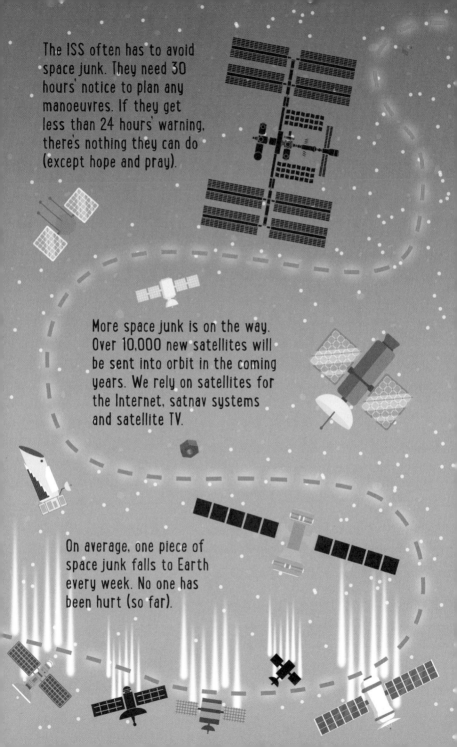

The ISS often has to avoid space junk. They need 30 hours' notice to plan any manoeuvres. If they get less than 24 hours' warning, there's nothing they can do (except hope and pray).

More space junk is on the way. Over 10,000 new satellites will be sent into orbit in the coming years. We rely on satellites for the Internet, satnav systems and satellite TV.

On average, one piece of space junk falls to Earth every week. No one has been hurt (so far).

In 2007, an airline pilot watched a piece of space junk from a Russian spy satellite drop out of the sky and narrowly miss his plane – and its 270 passengers.

In a few hundred years, scientists believe we'll all be trapped on Earth, unable to leave because of all the space junk!

This is why there are plans to clear the junk up. NASA are developing a giant sheet called Brane Craft that will fold itself around any junk and drag it back down to Earth, where it will crash and burn in the Earth's atmosphere.

Bye folks!

SOURCES

This book wouldn't have been possible without a huge number of AWESOME books and websites.
Here are just a few of my favourites:

BRILLIANT BOOKS:
Death by Black Hole and other Cosmic Quandries (Neil DeGrasse Tyson, 2007)
Astrophysics for People in a Hurry (Neil DeGrasse Tyson, 2017)
We Have No Idea: A Guide to the Unknown Universe
(Jorge Cham and Daniel Whiteson, 2017)
DK Knowledge Encyclopaedia: Space (DK, 2015)
Space: From Earth to the Edge of the Universe (DK, 2010)
A User's Guide to the Universe (Dave Goldberg and Jeff Blomquist, 2010)
Is There Life on Mars? The 20 Big Universe Questions (Stuart Clark, 2014)
1139 QI Facts to Make Your Jaw Drop (John Lloyd and John Mitchinson, 2013)
The QI Books of General Ignorance (John Lloyd and John Mitchinson, 2006 – 2017)
The Horrible Science Books (Nick Arnold and Tony De Saulles, 1996 – 2017)
An Astronaut's Guide to Life on Earth (Chris Hadfield Macmillan, 2013)
The Usborne Official Astronaut's Handbook (Louie Stowell and Roger Simo, 2015)
A Universe from Nothing (Lawrence M. Krauss, 2012)
We Need to Talk About Kelvin (Marcus Chown, 2009)

WONDERFUL WEBSITES:
nasa.gov
qi.com
britannica.com
kids.nationalgeographic.com
BBC, The Guardian, The Independent, The Telegraph
and The New York Times websites and QI Elves on Twitter.

And, of course, Google.